SACRED
MARRIAGE

D0469826

PARTICIPANT'S GUIDE

Books by Gary Thomas

Authentic Faith

Devotions for a Sacred Marriage

Devotions for Sacred Parenting

The Glorious Pursuit

Holy Available

Not the End but the Road

Sacred Influence

Sacred Marriage

Sacred Parenting

Sacred Pathways

Seeking the Face of God

SACRED MARRIAGE

WHAT IF GOD DESIGNED MARRIAGE TO MAKE US HOLY MORE THAN TO MAKE US HAPPY?

PARTICIPANT'S GUIDE

GARY THOMAS

WITH KEVIN AND SHERRY HARNEY

ZONDERVAN.com/
AUTHOR**TRACKER**
follow your favorite authors

ZONDERVAN

Sacred Marriage Participant's Guide
Copyright © 2009 by Gary L. Thomas

Requests for information should be addressed to:
Zondervan, *Grand Rapids, Michigan 49530*

ISBN 978-0-310-29146-6

Interior design by Christine Orejuela-Winkelman

Printed in the United States of America

11 12 13 14 15 • 26 25 24 23 22 21 20 19 18 17 16 15 14 13 12 11 10 9 8 7 6

CONTENTS

A Word from Gary Thomas

In one of the sessions in this study, you'll hear me recount a time when my wife and I began a vacation with radically different agendas. Neither one of us was very happy with the resulting compromise; I didn't get near the amount of rest and recovery I was hoping for, and Lisa didn't get to see half the places she wanted to see, but you know what?

Maybe God's agenda wasn't for me to get all the rest I thought I needed, or for my wife to get all the excitement she desired. Maybe God wanted to confront the pride that rules both our hearts; he may well have been far more interested in both of us being shaped into the image of Christ than in having our immediate perceived needs met. Scripture teaches us that our goal should be to "do nothing out of selfish ambition or vain conceit, but in humility consider others better than yourselves. Each of you should look not only to your own interests, but also to the interests of others. Your attitude should be the same as that of Christ Jesus" (Philippians 2:3 – 5).

In this passage Paul tells us that selfishness can't be managed, it needs to be crucified, and that Christlikeness is one of the goals of our journey together. A needs-based approach to marriage will usually spawn resentment, frustration, bitterness, and alienation when we discover the other person can't truly meet our needs as we would like them to. But if we're looking for something else in our marriage — spiritual growth, a place to learn how to love, an opportunity to have our sin revealed so that it can be confessed, repented of, and discarded — then we'll value even the frustrating aspects of this intense relationship.

I've found that many couples think they resent each *other*, when in fact what they really resent is *marriage* — which I believe God specifically designed to "pinch our feet." The lifelong relationship between a man and a woman is tailor-made by our Creator to teach us about selflessness, forgiveness, perseverance, humility, and many other necessary virtues. We may not initially get married in pursuit of such character transformation, but when we begin to *embrace* marriage as the threshold to spiritual growth, many good things will result. It's not until we crucify our pride and take on the same attitude as that of Christ Jesus that we can participate in marriage as God designed it — as a human relationship between two sinners in which our Redeemer hopes to fashion two saints.

It's my belief that for too long, the Christian church has adopted a "monastic" model of spirituality that is all but blind to the powerfully soul-transforming aspects of married and family life. My prayer is that this study will help you view your marriage through an entirely new prism: a way to worship God, your heavenly "Father-in-Law" (you'll learn about that in session three), and a path through which he can shape you into a man or woman who more closely resembles Jesus Christ.

OF NOTE

Quotations interspersed throughout each session of this participant's guide are excerpts from the book *Sacred Marriage* by Gary Thomas (Zondervan, 2000).

SESSION 1

GOD'S PURPOSE FOR MARRIAGE: MORE THAN WE IMAGINE

God desires that we use the challenges, joys, struggles, and celebrations of marriage to draw closer to him and to grow in Christian character.

INTRODUCTION

This DVD study series, based on Gary Thomas's bestselling book of the same name, points beyond marriage. It is really about spiritual growth. Marriage is one powerful context in which God shapes us more into the image of Jesus.

Some people see marriage as a romantic fusion of souls and bodies. Others see it as a responsibility or a chore ... a commitment to perform a series of duties for another person. Still others see it as their best highway to happiness. In this session we will discover that God's design for marriage is richer and deeper than any of these perspectives.

Marriage has a sacred purpose. The intimacy and closeness of two married people creates a perfect setting for growth, maturing, and lessons in holiness. If we approach marriage with the right perspective and attitude, it can be one of the most glorious pursuits in all of life. If we come with the wrong outlook, it can quickly deteriorate into a place of pain, frustration, self-centered loneliness, and deep brokenness.

Building a strong marriage is one of the greatest challenges in the world. Yet, when we listen to the wisdom God has to offer, it can be a satisfying and life-changing journey that shapes our souls and connects us with God and each other.

TALK ABOUT IT

Before you walked the aisle and said, "I do," what was your perception of married life? How has that perception changed over the years?

DVD TEACHING NOTES

Introduction: To be single or married? That is the question.

The contrast between seeing marriage as a romantic pursuit or a spiritual journey

The cultural development of romantic notions and expectations in marriage

Marriage for the glory of God

   1.

   2.

   3.

A new mind-set: Do I need a new marriage or a new perspective on marriage?

DVD DISCUSSION

1. When a couple is married and live in continual close proximity, the littlest and strangest things can cause irritation and petty frustration. Tell about a time in your marriage when something small or strange happened that stripped away the well-designed façades to expose the real and sinful you.

2. What is one virtue or character quality you realized needed to grow more in your life once you got married?

3. Most of us get very little training to prepare for marriage. When it comes to the spiritual dynamics of marriage, there is often no preparation at all. What do you wish you had learned before taking your vows and beginning your marriage relationship?

If you are afraid to face your sin, don't get married because this relationship will expose your sin like nothing else.

4. Gary suggests that marriage might be meant to make us holy more than happy. Do you agree or disagree, and why?

The state of marriage is one that requires more virtue and constancy than any other ... it is a perpetual exercise in mortification.... From this thyme plant, in spite of the bitter nature of its juice, you may be able to draw and make the honey of a holy life.

Francis de Sales

5. Some couples live with a conviction that their marriage relationship is designed to meet their needs, satisfy their hunger for ever-increasing romance, and fill the void they feel in their heart and soul. How do you see this concept being promoted in modern culture? What are some of the possible consequences of viewing marriage this way?

6. When things get tough, why are many people swift to think they married the wrong person rather than concluding that their idealized notion of marriage might be inaccurate or unbiblical?

If we find that the same kinds of challenges face every marriage, we might assume that God designed a purpose in this challenge that transcends something as illusory as happiness.

7. Read at least two of the following Bible passages, then respond to the related question:

   a. *1 Corinthians 10:31.* How might your marriage change if you believed you are meant to be married for the glory of God?

   b. *Genesis 2:20 – 25.* How is marriage part of God's design and plan for people?

c. *Matthew 6:33*. How can the focus of a marriage change if we seek God first and look for him to be the primary source of satisfaction and joy in our life?

d. *Romans 8:28 – 29*. God is deeply concerned about conforming us into the image of Jesus. How can a marriage relationship be the perfect setting for God to do this?

8. Gary says marriage can be an ideal place to learn lessons such as forgiveness, patience, and understanding. Tell one story, as a couple, about how God has grown one of these characteristics in your lives because you are married to each other.

If people get married for a reason as trivial as a romantic high, they will probably end up getting divorced for something as trivial as the loss of romantic intensity!

CLOSING

Take time as a group (or as couples) to pray in some of the following directions:

- Father, teach me humility so that I can see how you want to grow me and shape me through my spouse.
- Give me wisdom to see when my view of marriage is based on a picture painted by the media or the world and not shaped by your Word and truth.
- Jesus, when I feel discouraged or disheartened, help me to remember all that you sacrificed for me. Give me strength to stand strong in my marriage, even when emotions ebb and frustration grows.
- God of hope, fill me with anticipation for all the good things you want to do in my marriage as we walk through this learning experience together.

Between Sessions

Couple's Conversation and Prayer

Take time before your next group meeting to talk and pray together about one or more of these topics:

- **Talk About It:** *Talk with your spouse about one or two big lessons that hit you during the DVD and discussion time with your group. What was one way your understanding of marriage was confirmed and supported? What was one way it was challenged? Share one thing you are hoping and praying God will do in your life through this Sacred Marriage learning experience.*

- **Pray About It:** *Pray together for a renewed and deeper commitment to your marriage. Ask the Spirit of God to protect you from riding the roller coaster of a marriage based on how a spouse is feeling at any given moment. Ask God to help you live with a tenacious, joyful expectancy for what God wants to do in your life through your marriage. With anticipation, pray for God to use your spouse, in any way that would honor Jesus, to mold and shape your life.*

- **Read and Reflect:** *Read Genesis 1:26 – 31 and Genesis 2:20 – 25 as a couple. What do you notice about the way God made men and women? What was God's plan and design for marriage before sin came into the picture? Was there anything in these passages that struck you in a fresh or new way?*

ACTIVITIES

Try one or more of the following suggestions:

- **Personal Exercise:** *Write a note to your spouse, expressing how you have seen them grow to look, act, and be more like Jesus. Also, write down one or two ways you have seen the marriage journey shape you more into the image of Jesus. Let your spouse know that you thank God for how he has used them in this refining and maturing process.*

- **Journaling Exercise:** *Identify one or two "little things" that tend to irritate and bug you. Then, either in a notebook or on the page provided at the end of this session, journal your responses to the following questions:*

  What are "little things" that tend to irritate me?

  Why do these things bother me so much?

  How can I release some of this irritation and learn to love and serve in deeper ways?

  How can embracing this process make me more like Jesus?

- **Personal Prayer:** *Invite the Spirit to search your heart and pray for the wisdom and self-control needed so that you will not spend the series nudging your spouse in the ribs with a sharp elbow. Pray that your focus, as you walk through this Sacred Marriage study, will be on what God wants to do in your life.*

RECOMMENDED READING

In preparation for session two, you may want to read chapter 8 of the book Sacred Marriage, *by Gary Thomas.*

Journal

SESSION 2

The Refining Power of Marriage

Marriage helps us to develop the character of God himself as we stick with our spouses through the good times and the bad. Every wedding gives birth to a new history, a new beginning. The spiritual meaning of marriage is found in maintaining that history together.

Introduction

In session one we examined the idea that God might just want to use marriage to make us holy even more than to make us happy. Of course, there are many joy-filled moments along the way, but God often uses the marriage relationship to forge our souls and strengthen our hearts.

In this session we look more closely at the refining power of the marriage relationship. One of God's best ways of shaping our character and growing our maturity is through relationships. And there is no human relationship with greater potential to accomplish this divine directive than marriage.

Every human being who has ever walked the face of this earth (except Jesus) battles with sin and brokenness. This means that every marriage is made up of two imperfect people. In light of this, we should not be shocked or surprised that marriage can be challenging at times. We should expect it. As we adjust our understanding of our spouse and who we are, we will discover that God can use this intimate relationship to refine, strengthen, and grow us in amazing ways.

TALK ABOUT IT

As you look back over your history as a married couple (be it short or long), what is an example of how God has used your spouse to make you a stronger person?

DVD TEACHING NOTES

Introduction: Marrying someone who stumbles in many ways

Abraham and Mary Todd Lincoln: How God shapes a person through marriage

God can strengthen character through the challenges of marriage

Training a thoroughbred, how God prepares us for the race

God can use our failings

How marriage can change over the years

DVD DISCUSSION

1. How does the simple truth of James 3:2 — "we all stumble in many ways" — impact a person who is waiting to get married until they find the "perfect person"?

2. How might this truth inform the decisions of a person who is considering leaving their spouse because they want to go in search of their "soul mate" who will help them form a perfect marriage with no struggles and disagreements?

If marriage is the union of one person who stumbles in many ways to another person who stumbles in many ways, occasionally having sex and making little people who stumble in many ways, why are so many people surprised when they discover how difficult marriage can be?

3. Abraham Lincoln is often ranked as one of the best presidents in American history. His wife, Mary Todd Lincoln, is often ranked quite low as a first lady. Yet Abraham stayed married to her even through times of great pain and struggle. When you think of the specific time in history in which Abraham Lincoln lived and led (during the Civil War), how might God have been using Mary Todd to help refine and shape her husband for the task before him?

4. What is one unique way God has wired you that has helped shape your spouse to be the person God wants him/her to be? And what is one characteristic in your spouse that God is using to shape you more into the man/woman God wants you to be? Think about Proverbs 27:17 — "As iron sharpens iron, so one man sharpens another" — in the context of marriage, even though the verse's application is broader than that.

The relationship between God and his people was anything but easy ... there were times of great joy and celebration, frustration and anger, infidelity and apostasy, and excruciating seasons of silence. Sound like any relationship you know? Your own marriage, for example?

5. Gary talks about how the breathtaking beauty of Mount Everest was created by Eurasia and India "crashing into each other" through countless years. What is one way you and your spouse have been "crashing into each other" over time in a way that has actually created something beautiful and honoring to God? How would your life and the world be a less beautiful place if God had not brought you into close proximity with your spouse and given you the gift of the consistent pressure of being married?

6. Tell about a season of life that you look back on as a couple and realize that God was preparing, training, and conditioning you for something greater and more significant than you realized at the time. If you had bailed out and quit when the conditioning got tough, what might you have missed out on as a couple?

Beautiful people don't just happen. Mature people are not an accident. It is a process. We are born sinners and have to be refined. People are one of God's tools to complete the refining process.

7. Gary makes a very provocative statement: "Most couples don't fall out of love … they fall out of repentance." He goes on to discuss how we can exhibit numerous virtues and practices before we are married that seem to dwindle once we are married and as the years pass. Why do you think people can behave one way before getting married and then a very different way after saying, "I do"?

8. What can help us maintain a high level of commitment to virtues such as kindness, generosity, serving, and forgiveness through the long journey of marriage?

9. When we are gripped by the reality that God can use the challenges of marriage to refine and grow us, our whole outlook changes. Picture the same person in the same marriage but with these very different outlooks:

   Option 1: The struggles and challenges of marriage surprise me every time they come. They are an inconvenience, an irritation, and something I don't want or deserve.

   Option 2: The struggles and challenges of marriage are a normal part of the journey. I don't delight in them, but I do know that these things will refine my soul, make me stronger, and prepare me to be the person God needs me to be.

What are some of the potential results in the life of this person with attitude number 1? What can you do to adopt an outlook more like option 2?

If we are serious about pursuing spiritual growth through marriage, we must convince ourselves to refrain from asking the spiritually dangerous question: "Did I marry the 'right' person?" Once we have exchanged our vows, little can be gained spiritually from ruminating on this question. A far better alternative to questioning one's choice is to learn how to live with one's choice.

CLOSING

Take time as a group (or as couples) to pray in some of the following directions:

- God of grace, help me to remember that both my spouse and I "stumble in many ways." Guard me from the folly of being surprised or shocked when marriage is difficult.
- Jesus, thank you for the grace you pour out freely on each of us. You know how we stumble and you still love us.
- Spirit of God, I invite you to use my spouse, however you like, to refine and grow me into the person you want me to be.
- God of hope, give us a new vision for all you want to do in each of us through our spouse. Replace resentment with anticipation.

Between Sessions

Couple's Conversation and Prayer

Take time before your next group meeting to talk and pray together about one or more of these topics:

- **Talk About It:** *Talk with your spouse about one or two big lessons that hit you during the DVD and discussion time with your group. Thank your spouse for the many ways God has used them to refine and grow you. Discuss how your marriage might become more hope-filled if you both determine to see the challenges you face as divine moments that can lead to maturity and growth.*

- **Pray About It:** *Pray together for hearts that are open to all God wants to do in you through times of challenge and difficulty. Thank God for your spouse and for how God has used them as a tool to grow your heart and faith. Confess where you have been resistant to God's work in your heart through your marriage. Also, confess where your view of marriage has been based on a worldly vision and not God's design.*

- **Read and Reflect:** *Read Romans 15:1–6 and 2 Corinthians 1:3–7 as a couple. What do you notice about God's desire for his people to grow in endurance? What characteristics mark the life of a person who is not committed to endure through the tough times? What kind of fruit do you see in the life of a couple who is committed to endure, even when things get tough?*

Activities

Try one or more of the following suggestions:

- **Personal Exercise:** *Over the coming week, evaluate your response to moments of conflict and tension in your marriage.*

When things get difficult, is your knee-jerk response to get frustrated and get out of the situation? Or, do you actually pause and ask God if there is something he wants to do in your heart and marriage through this challenging situation? Make a commitment to pause in these pivotal times to ask God to accomplish his will in your life.

- **Journaling Exercise:** *Do a Mount Everest reflection time. Think back through the history of your relationship with your spouse and identify the seasons when there have been lots of "crashing into each other." Also, identify the recurring points of friction that have endured through the years of your marriage. Then, either in a notebook or on the page provided at the end of this session, write about any or all of the following themes:*

    What are some of our points of recurring tension and conflict? What has God grown in me through these experiences?

    How am I a better person and more equipped for God's plan for my life because of these experiences in my marriage?

    What are some of the majestic and beautiful Mount Everest peaks that are forming in our lives because we have endured over time and allowed God to accomplish his work in us?

- **Personal Prayer:** *Confess where you have been resistant and even bitter over the struggles you have faced in your marriage. Ask for a new outlook that is captured by God's vision of shaping you into his person through your marriage relationship. Pray for patience and strength as you learn to see the struggles of marriage as a gift rather than a curse.*

RECOMMENDED READING

In preparation for session three, you may want to read chapters 2 and 10 in the book Sacred Marriage, by Gary Thomas.

Journal

SESSION 3

THE GOD-CENTERED SPOUSE

To become a servant is to become radically strong spiritually. It means you are free from the petty demands and grievances that ruin so many lives and turn so many hearts into bitter cauldrons of disappointment, self-absorption, and self-pity.

INTRODUCTION

What will a marriage look like if both parties are self-centered? Just imagine the frustration as competing desires conflict!

What if each spouse centers their focus on the other? Each one seeks to love, serve, and do what would bring joy to their spouse. This kind of spouse-centered relationship will be much healthier and will come closer to God's design for marriage.

Now imagine a marriage that moves beyond self-centered motivation and past a spouse-centered focus. What might this covenant relationship become if both husband and wife were God-centered in their marriage? How might love increase, service flow, and forgiveness be extended if the focus of our marriage became based on acting out of reverence for God?

TALK ABOUT IT

Tell about a time in your marriage when you both discovered that your needs, interests, or desires were dramatically different. How could these differences create bumps along the road of marriage if you are not sensitive to them?

DVD TEACHING NOTES

Introduction: Hawaii ... a laboratory for discovering differences

The problems that arise in a need-based marriage

Perfecting holiness and purifying ourselves

> *Since we have these promises, dear friends, let us purify ourselves from everything that contaminates body and spirit, perfecting holiness out of reverence for God.*
>
> 2 Corinthians 7:1

Loving each other out of reverence for Christ

The doctrine of God as Father-in-Law: the radical nature of God's love

> *As humans with finite minds, we need the power of symbolism in order to gain understanding. By means of the simple relationship of a man and a woman, the symbol of marriage can call up virtually infinite meaning. This will happen only when we use our marriage to explore God. If we are consumed with highlighting where our spouses are falling short, we will miss diving into the mysteries of marriage and the lessons it has to teach us.*

DVD DISCUSSION

1. Think about a time in your marriage when your needs were not met and you responded by withholding something (communication, romance, intimacy, finances, affirmation, etc.) from your spouse. How did this "withholding" approach impact your relationship?

2. Read 2 Corinthians 7:1 (it's on page 34 if you don't have a Bible handy). Little sins can creep into a marriage and we hardly notice them. A desire to grow in purity and to perfect holiness can shine God's light into the dark corners of our hearts and lives. Describe a time that the holy light of God's presence began to shine in your life and you saw a "little" habit, pattern, or behavior you had not noticed before. How has that habit, pattern, or behavior changed since God brought it into the light?

The apostle Paul is crystal clear: the first question we should ask ourselves when doing anything is, "Will this be pleasing to Jesus Christ?" The first purpose in marriage — beyond happiness, sexual expression, the bearing of children, companionship, mutual care and provision, or anything else — is to please God.

3. If our primary motivation to love and serve our spouse is based on how they have treated us in the past forty-eight hours, how might this impact the way we offer *one* of the following:

   • Physical care

   • Verbal encouragement

- Acts of service

- Emotional engagement

- Some other aspect of the marriage relationship

4. If our primary motivation to love and serve our spouse is based on an authentic desire to show reverence for Jesus, how might this impact the way we offer *one* of the following:

- Physical care

- Verbal encouragement

- Acts of service

- Emotional engagement

- Some other aspect of the marriage relationship

5. Choose one or two areas of the marriage relationship (there are a few listed below) and contrast what this area might look like if a person is: self-centered, spouse-centered, or God-centered.

Area of Marriage	If a Mate Is Self-Centered	If a Mate Is Spouse-Centered	If a Mate Is God-Centered
How finances are handled			
How forgiveness is extended			
How communication is maintained			
How free time is used			
How family of origin issues are navigated			

6. Gary talked about the moment it hit him that God is not only his Father, but his Father-in-Law. If we lived with a profound awareness that our husband or wife is a precious and loved child of God and that our heavenly Father-in-Law cares deeply about how we treat them, how might this impact the way we care for our spouse?

Years ago Paul Simon wrote a bestselling song proclaiming "Fifty Ways to Leave Your Lover." A Christian needs just one reason to stay with his or her "lover": the analogy of Christ and his church.

7. If your heavenly Father-in-Law came to your group and told you about his love and affection for your spouse, what might he say? Remember, he sees them as his child ... his loved son or daughter.

8. How might loving your spouse out of reverence for God *stop* you from doing something you otherwise might do?

9. Read Luke 6:32 – 33 and Matthew 5:43 – 44. What do these passages have to say to those who give love to their spouse based on what they get from their spouse? How does Jesus blow up our conventional understanding of love being about what we get and how we feel?

> Marriage creates a situation in which our desire to be served and coddled can be replaced with a more noble desire to serve others — even to sacrifice for others. This is a call for both husbands and wives. The beauty of marriage is that it confronts our selfishness and demands our service twenty-four hours a day. When we're most tired, most worn down, and feeling more sorry for ourselves than we ever have before, we have the opportunity to confront feelings of self-pity by getting up and serving our mate.

CLOSING

Take time as a group (or as couples) to pray in some of the following directions:

- Please teach me to center myself fully on you, dear God, even in my marriage.
- Dear Jesus, forgive me for the times I have been self-centered in my marriage. Teach me to serve my spouse out of reverence for you.
- Heavenly Father-in-Law, help me to see my husband/wife as your loved and precious child. Teach me to love them in a way that will bring joy to their Father's heart!
- You are holy, holy, holy! I pray that you will help me grow in purity and holiness in every area of life, including in my marriage relationship.

One of the reasons I am determined to keep my marriage together is not because doing so will make me happier (although I believe it will); not because I want my kids to have a secure home (although I do desire that); not because it would tear me up to see my wife have to "start over" (although it would). The first reason I keep my marriage together is because it is my Christian duty. If my life is based on proclaiming God's message to the world, I don't want to do anything that would challenge that message.

BETWEEN SESSIONS

COUPLE'S CONVERSATION AND PRAYER

Take time before your next group meeting to talk and pray together about one or more of these topics:

- **Talk About It:** *Talk with your spouse about one or two big lessons that hit you during the DVD and discussion time with your group. Also, brainstorm new patterns and actions you can infuse into your marriage that will show the Father that you love his son or daughter (your spouse).*

- **Pray About It:** *Pray together for a marriage that is not based on the needs of the other as much as it is based on reverence for God. Ask God to help you see, in the core of your hearts, that you will both be more loved and more satisfied in your marriage if each of you is God-centered more than spouse-centered. Thank your heavenly Father-in-Law for his child (your spouse) and lift up specific things about him/her that delight the Father and you.*

- **Read and Reflect:** *Read Isaiah 62:5; Hosea 2:16–20; Matthew 22:1–2; and Revelation 19:7. Over and over God uses the husband and wife as a picture of his relationship with his people. Why do you think God does this? What are some of the parallels you see between a marriage of a man and a woman and God's relationship with his children?*

ACTIVITIES

Try one or more of the following suggestions:

- **Personal Exercise:** *Identify an area in your marriage where you are withholding love, care, or something else because your spouse is not meeting your need or doing what you want. Now look at this same area through the lens of loving your spouse out of reverence for Christ. How might you adjust the way you are treating your wife/husband if your primary motivation is to bring glory to God?*

- **Journaling Exercise:** *Use Philippians 2:1–8 as a launch pad into your journal time. Read the passage, then record (either in a notebook or on the page provided at the end of this session) some of the ways your attitude and actions might change if you followed this counsel of the apostle Paul and the example of Jesus.*

- **Personal Prayer:** *Ask Christ to help you base the way you treat your spouse on your reverence for him, not on what your spouse does or does not do. Ask the Spirit of God to grow you in holiness and purity as you learn to love your spouse. Invite the Father to teach you to see your spouse the way he does, as a loved and cherished child.*

RECOMMENDED READING

In preparation for session four, you may want to read chapter 7 of the book Sacred Marriage, *by Gary Thomas.*

Journal

SESSION 4

SACRED HISTORY

One characteristic holds the history of God and Israel together—perseverance. When Israel turned her back on God, God didn't turn his back on Israel.

INTRODUCTION

Throughout history, God has walked with his people. When the children of God have stayed close to the heart of their heavenly Father, he has delighted in their love. In seasons of rebellion and wandering, God has disciplined, wooed, and invited his children to come back home, but he has never abandoned them. From the highs to the lows in the histories of Israel and the church, God has remained steadfast in his love and unyielding in his devotion.

This picture of God's faithfulness to his people over the long haul gives a helpful image for couples desiring to build a sacred history in their marriage. If we are going to mirror the heart of God in our marriage relationship, it will be a marathon — not a sprint. It means committing to hang in there when things get tough, celebrating when things are going well, being devoted when emotions ebb low, and giving God the glory in the times of harmony, joy, and inexpressible delight. It means taking seriously the promise to love your spouse for better *and* for worse, in times of plenty *and* want, in sickness *and* in health … as long as you both shall live.

These aren't just nice words for a wedding ceremony. They are the pathway to writing a sacred history.

TALK ABOUT IT

What was one of the lines in your wedding vows that spoke of committing to your spouse no matter what you faced together? Why do you think most wedding vows include these kinds of promises?

DVD TEACHING NOTES

Introduction: Israel's sacred history and the journey of a marriage
    Joy and celebration
    Frustration and anger
    Failure and brokenness
    Excruciating times of silence and struggle
    God's presence through it all
    God's divine design

Characteristics of a good marriage and a good spiritual life

The value of perseverance

The fundamentals: The real-life story of John Wooden

DVD DISCUSSION

1. As you think of the history of God and his people as recorded in the Bible, note aloud some of the various seasons in the relationships — joyful times, frustrating times, broken times, even silent times. How does this mirror the journey of a husband and wife?

2. Why is it important to honestly acknowledge that every marriage will have seasons of incredible intimacy and painful distance, of romantic bliss and relational tension?

Whatever season of marriage we find ourselves in, we can profit from it because it so closely mirrors God's relationship with Israel.

3. For much of human history, due to short life spans, most marriages built a history that only spanned one to three decades. Today a couple can look forward to four, five, or even six decades of married life. What are some of the realities that settle in when a couple realizes they might just be spending half a century together?

4. Gary notes how recent studies of the human brain have taught us that it can take from a decade to fifteen years for a couple to truly create the deepest of bonds and have a sense of being one. If this is how God has designed the brain to work, how might this reality influence *one* of the following situations:

    - A newlywed couple that is four months into their marriage and feels they might not be right for each other because they are still struggling with differences

    - A couple that is dealing with the "seven-year itch" and wondering if the grass might be greener on the other side of the fence

    - A husband and wife who have three kids under the age of five and can't figure out why they don't feel the same romantic intensity and sense of oneness they enjoyed when they started dating

Building a sacred history together teaches us to be persistent in doing good, even when we want to do something else. This commitment to perseverance teaches us the basic Christian discipline of self-denial.

5. The very things we need for a healthy marriage are what we need for a growing walk of faith: commitment, tenacity, loyalty, and willingness to hang in there when times get tough. How can a vibrant and growing faith in Jesus strengthen your marriage? How can an unyielding commitment to love and serve your spouse, even when things get difficult, strengthen your relationship with Jesus?

6. Gary cites a well-known Hollywood actress — a woman who has gone through a number of marriages, engagements, and boyfriends — whose philosophy of life is, "You have to be happy in the moment!" Read James 1:4. How does James' teaching and the philosophy of this woman paint differing views of life and happiness?

God knows how he has designed us and how slow the process of building true intimacy can be. That is why his plan is one marriage to one person for a lifetime.

7. In a case study, researchers worked with couples who described their marriage experience as "severely dissatisfying" or "very severely dissatisfying." Five years later, most of the couples who chose to remain married described their marriage as "very satisfying." Of those who pursued divorce, only 17 percent said they were satisfied with their current relationship. These objective findings fly in the face of conventional wisdom that encourages us to leave a challenging marriage so we can find true happiness. How would you explain these results?

8. Building a sacred history means hanging in there during the challenging seasons of marriage. Talk about some of the challenges a couple might face in *one* of the following seasons and how they can hold on to each other and the hand of God during these times:

   • The years when children are born and you have a young and growing family

- Years that you would love to have kids, but are not able to conceive

- Seasons of financial stress and strain when it is hard to make ends meet

- When you are raising teens and they are testing boundaries

- The empty nest years when kids move out and you have more time to look at each other than you have had in decades

- When your parents are getting on in years and need more of your help and support

9. Gary told the story of John Wooden, the legendary basketball coach at UCLA who was also an amazing example of devotion to his wife. Tell about a couple you have had the honor of watching write a beautiful sacred history together, and one lesson you have learned from this couple.

WISE WORDS FROM JOHN WOODEN

Be more concerned with your character than your reputation, because your character is what you really are, while your reputation is merely what others think you are.

It's the little details that are vital. Little things make big things happen.

There are many things that are essential to arriving at true peace of mind, and one of the most important is faith, which cannot be acquired without prayer.

CLOSING

Take time as a group (or as couples) to pray in some of the following directions:

- God, grow hearts of perseverance in each of us so we can write a sacred history with each other and with you.
- Help us, in the difficult times, to remember that this is part of the journey and you are always with us.
- Thank you for those who have been models of passionate perseverance and loving commitment in their marriage.
- Father, be with those we care about who are in a challenging season of marriage. Help them hold on to you and each other as they press through.

There are seasons of life that can rock your intimacy. Couples who persevere to the end discover an even deeper level of intimacy.

BETWEEN SESSIONS

COUPLE'S CONVERSATION AND PRAYER

Take time before your next group meeting to talk and pray together about one or more of these topics:

- **Talk About It:** *Talk with your spouse about one or two big lessons that hit you during the DVD and discussion time with your group. Review the history you have written so far. What were some of the wonderful times filled with joy, laughter, and great memories? What were some of the challenging times, and how did God bring you through them? How can you draw from the tough times in the past to be strong for what you might face in the future?*

- **Pray About It:** *Together ask the Holy Spirit to infuse you with tenacious perseverance and a growing commitment to your marriage, no matter what life throws at you. Thank God for the good times and acknowledge that these have been a gift of his grace. Pray for other couples you care about ... ask God to help them develop their own sacred history.*

- **Read and Reflect:** *Read Romans 5:1 – 5; Hebrews 12:1 – 3; and James 1:2 – 8 as a couple. What is God saying about the place of perseverance in the life of a Christian? What lessons can you draw from these passages into your marriage as you seek to write a sacred history of your own?*

ACTIVITIES

Try one or more of the following suggestions:

- **Personal Exercise:** *Write a note to a couple that has been a model of faithfulness and perseverance for you. Describe how your life and marriage have been impacted by their example.*

- **Journaling Exercise:** *In a notebook or on the page provided at the end of this session, reflect on how God has helped you through the challenging times of marriage. Refer to the list in question eight (pages 50–51) to identify possible areas to focus your journaling. How has God been with you, carried you through, and given strength along the way?*

- **Personal Prayer:** *Thank God for his story of faithfulness and constancy taught in the Bible. Give him praise for loving the people of Israel through their history. Thank him for his great love for the church. Then, celebrate his unfailing love for you and your spouse. Bless him for walking with you through your history, be it short or long. Close by inviting him to lead you, as a couple, for all the years that are ahead.*

RECOMMENDED READING

In preparation for session five, you may want to read chapter 11 in the book Sacred Marriage, by Gary Thomas.

Journal

SESSION 5

SEXUAL SAINTS

May your fountain be blessed, and may you rejoice in the wife of your youth. A loving doe, a graceful deer—may her breasts satisfy you always, may you ever be captivated by her love.

Proverbs 5:18–19

INTRODUCTION

When it comes to sex, all kinds of misconceptions are floating around. If we look at popular culture we will see sex presented as a recreational activity focused on self-satisfaction, nothing more than an instinctual animal response to another person. Morality, boundaries, and the marital commitment are tossed aside and people feel free to express their sexuality in any and every way imaginable. In the church some people get the impression that sex is bad, dirty, and something to be avoided. At best, it's a necessary evil, but let's keep it in the dark where it belongs. The idea of preaching about sexuality or celebrating it as a good gift is not even on the radar of many Christians.

A biblical view of sex flies in the face of these two extremes. Human sexuality and the very act of sex are wonderful gifts from the Creator who made a man and woman, placed them in a garden, and said, "Be fruitful and multiply." In Genesis we are told that Adam and Eve were "both naked, and they felt no shame." Within the context of the marriage covenant, sex is meant to be enjoyed by a husband and a wife. Christians should not blush or be embarrassed to talk about sex. The truth is, we are God's sexual saints!

TALK ABOUT IT

What formed your view of human sexuality as you were growing up? How close was your view to the biblical idea that sex is a good gift from God when it is expressed in the marriage relationship between a man and a woman?

DVD TEACHING NOTES

Introduction: The Bible and sexuality

The power of sexual fulfillment and the danger of sexual addictions

How sex is spiritually formative in a marriage:
1. A healthy sexual relationship creates a bridge for greater spiritual, emotional, and relational intimacy
2. A healthy sexual relationship grows a spirit of giving
3. A healthy sexual relationship teaches us about building hearts of faithfulness

DVD Discussion

1. Read Genesis 2:22 – 25; Song of Songs chapter 7; and Proverbs 5:15 – 19. Some Christians view sex as something to be ignored or avoided, or they believe that "good" Christians don't talk about such things. How does the teaching of the Bible confront this perspective on human sexuality?

2. Gary says, "A man who is sexually fulfilled is a better father, husband, worker, and even a better Christian." He says, "The reverse is also true. One of the best ways to zap a man's strength is to give him a sexual addiction or for him to be involved in any kind of sexual expression outside of his marriage." How do you respond to these statements, and what are some of the implications if Gary is right?

God doesn't turn his eyes when a married couple goes to bed. It only stands to reason that we shouldn't turn our eyes from God when we share intimate moments with our spouse.

3. Of the many spiritual benefits to a healthy sexual relationship between a husband and a wife, one is that the physical urge for sexual intimacy becomes a motivator for keeping the spiritual, relational, and emotional parts of the marriage healthy and growing. In God's design, a man never feels closer to his wife than right after they have experienced sexual intercourse. How does this reality speak to a husband's needs and motivation for being intimate with his wife? How does this speak to the way a wife understands what drives and motivates her husband?

4. Between the messages being pounded into our minds by a sex-saturated culture and our own tendency toward selfishness, it would be easy to view sex as a purely self-serving activity. But God sees this time of intimacy between a husband and wife as an opportunity for us to grow as servants. What are some ways a husband and wife can serve one another in the sexual area of their relationship, and how might a commitment to sexual servanthood grow a marriage?

The only sexual life a Christian spouse can legitimately enjoy is the romantic life a spouse chooses to provide. This makes manipulation and rejection ever-present spectators in the marital bed. Anything denied physically becomes an absolute denial, because there is no other legitimate outlet. (On the other hand, placing an unbearable sexual burden on a spouse in an attempt to meet other, unfulfilled needs can also be a manipulating abuse of power.)

5. Read John 13:2 – 5, 12 – 16. Jesus was the most powerful person to ever walk this earth, and he chose to serve. How does his example speak to the way a Christian husband and wife should treat each other in every area of their relationship, including in the bedroom?

6. Respond to this statement: "In a marriage relationship, whoever wants sex the least has the most power in bed." What does this say to the spouse who wants sex more and to the spouse who wants sex less?

Becoming more like Jesus is the essence of Christianity and none of us can say with any degree of sincerity that we have cornered the market on being a servant. Our marriages provide opportunities every day for us to be pushed further in this direction.

7. Gary says the most typical sexual sin for a man is to become a voyeur (looking at and lusting after many women, desiring to be satisfied by women in general and not just one woman — his wife). And the most typical sexual sin for a woman is to become an exhibitionist (dressing immodestly and becoming flirtatious because she wants to be adored by men in general and not just one man — her husband). If a husband or wife is engaging in this kind of behavior, what are some of the ways this might impact the marriage both inside and outside of the bedroom?

8. Just as snacks before dinner can ruin our appetite for good food, filling our eyes with impure images or our minds with romantic novels or movies can ruin our appetite for the intimacy of the marriage bed. How can we cut off the sources of unhealthy sexuality our society places in front of us so that our hunger for intimacy with our spouse will grow?

Every hunger that entices us in the flesh is an exploitation of a need that can be better met by God. The only context for godly sex is marital sex.

CLOSING

Take time as a group (or as couples) to pray in some of the following directions:

- Thank you for the good gift of sexuality and for the perfect setting to express it, the marriage relationship.
- Help us to see that sexual intimacy is a bridge to growing closer in every area of our relationship, including our emotional and spiritual connections.
- Teach us how to be generous servants in how we care for our spouses in every area of our marriage, including in the bedroom.

To fully embrace marital sexuality and all that God designed it for, couples must bring their Christianity into the bedroom and break down the wall between their physical and spiritual intimacy.

BETWEEN SESSIONS

COUPLE'S CONVERSATION AND PRAYER

Take time before your next group meeting to talk and pray together about one or more of these topics:

- **Talk About It:** *Talk with your spouse about one or two big lessons that hit you during the DVD and discussion time with your group. Have an honest conversation about what will lead to a stronger sexual connection between you. Use some of the questions below to guide your conversation. Remember, be honest, but gentle.*

  What do I do that makes you feel loved and valued?

  What makes you feel distant and disconnected from me?

  When we are sexually intimate, what brings you the greatest physical pleasure?

  Is there anything we do that is not pleasurable or that makes you feel uncomfortable?

  How can I serve you more consistently in the bedroom and out of the bedroom?

- **Pray About It:** *Together ask God to help you see sexuality and sexual intimacy through his eyes ... as a good gift to be enjoyed in the context of marriage. Ask him to bring to light any unhealthy behavior or life-pattern in relationship to your sexuality, and that you'll have eyes to see and a heart that is ready to repent and turn from these actions. Ask Jesus to help you learn from his example of humble service. Pray that you will learn to serve your spouse with tender care, inside and outside of the bedroom.*

- **Read and Reflect:** *Read some portions of Song of Songs to each other. Husbands, read the following portions to your bride: 4:1–7 and 7:1–9. Wives, read the following passages to your groom: 2:3–13 and 5:10–16. How might you express some of the ideas in these passages in language more appropriate to our time? How did it feel to speak words of deep affection and intimacy to each other?*

Activities

Try one or more of the following suggestions:

- **Personal Exercise:** *This week, make a point of watching your patterns and behavior. Men: Identify when your eyes wander to other women, when you are drawn to a TV show, movie, or Internet site that might lessen your appetite for your spouse. Women: Notice when you read novels, watch movies, or indulge in anything that is designed to fill your longing for romance. As you identify these patterns, offer them to God and seek to cut off these sources that kill your desire for the true love of your life — your spouse.*

- **Journaling Exercise:** *In a notebook or on the page provided at the end of this session, reflect on these questions: If God looked at nothing other than how I treat his daughter in bed (or for women, how you treat his son in bed) would he say that I am a mature Christian operating with the virtues of Christ — love, patience, purity, kindness, and generosity? If he only looked at this part of my life, would God be pleased?*

- **Personal Prayer:** *Confess where you have crossed lines with your sexuality. If you have become a voyeur or an exhibitionist, even in a "small" way, admit this to God and ask for his grace. Pray also for the power of the Holy Spirit to help you live in holiness and purity. Pray that the process of cutting off sinful patterns and* *sources of unhealthy sexual fulfillment will cause you to desire the goodness of sex enjoyed with your spouse in your covenant relationship.*

RECOMMENDED READING

In preparation for session six, you may want to read chapter 3 in the book Sacred Marriage, *by Gary Thomas.*

Journal

SESSION 6

MARRIAGE: THE LOVE LABORATORY

Most of us got married, not to learn how to love but to be loved.

INTRODUCTION

If God's plan for marriage was to simply make us happy, content, and comfortable, most of us would agree that something went wrong!

If God's intention for marriage was to create a laboratory where we could learn to love, be patient, and offer daily sacrifices of service, we would have to agree that he hit the mark.

There is no better place to learn the way of love than within the bounds of the marriage relationship. This close proximity to another person who is so different creates a furnace that will refine our character, melt our pride, and purify our motives. Every time God calls a man and woman to leave their family of origin, enter the realm of holy matrimony, and start a whole new life together, a new experiment begins.

Just as coal with time and intense pressure becomes a diamond, so marriage has the potential to form us into something more beautiful than we dream. This glorious relationship turns us into something far more valuable and precious than a diamond. It shapes us into the image of Jesus.

TALK ABOUT IT

What is one way you and your spouse are fundamentally different, and how has God used this to grow the character and heart of Jesus in you?

DVD TEACHING NOTES

Introduction: His brain, her brain

How the marriage relationship can teach us to love

Marriage addresses our deepest needs ...
    Husbands: to overcome our selfishness
    Wives: to overcome our disappointment
    My "soul mate" or my "sole mate"?

The story of Brian and Haley

DVD DISCUSSION

1. According to Gary, neurologists have discovered that the average woman processes complex emotional data up to seven times faster than the average man. What challenges might this bring to a marriage, and how have you seen this live itself out in your own?

2. What are some of the common motivations people have for getting married and how do these match up with what you have discovered to be the realities of the marriage relationship?

Common Motivations to Get Married	Reality You Have Experienced

If God's design for marriage is to teach us how to love and be less selfish, you can see how our desires and God's desires might conflict. Until we align ourselves with God's purpose for marriage, we may not only resent our spouse, we might ultimately resent marriage itself because it seems designed to put us in situations where our selfishness is confronted.

3. When a couple realizes that much of what they had hoped to get out of their marriage relationship turned out to be a mirage, what possible courses of action are available to them? How have you seen people respond when they came to understand that marriage will not provide all they had dreamed it would?

4. Gary tells of the time his wife wanted to visit some "cute shops" right when he wanted to watch a big sports event on TV. Husbands, in all honesty, what would be your typical response to this kind of request from your wife? Wives, how might you react to his response? How can such situations become a laboratory for learning love, for both a husband and wife?

> *When we grow in our commitment to serve each other, we become more like Jesus who said, "The Son of Man did not come to be served, but to serve" (Matthew 20:28).*

5. Read Ephesians 5:25. Gary says that God's design for marriage helps us confront our fundamental weaknesses, one of which is selfishness. How is marriage a perfect laboratory for learning to overcome our tendency to be selfish, and what is one story that illustrates this from your life?

6. Many people today believe there is one perfect person out there for them — a soul mate. Gary asks, "Do you really believe that God would base your future happiness and a lifetime of fulfillment on your ability, in your early to mid twenties, to find the one person out of over six billion people on the face of this earth with whom you can be successfully and intimately matched for the rest of your life? Do you think God would base your happiness on something that precarious? Does that sound like God to you?" What is the heart of the issue here, and how would you respond to Gary's questions?

> *Instead of looking for our "soul mate" I like to talk about our "sole mate." If marriage is about learning to love, it's about learning to walk out the biblical mandate to grow in love.*

7. Often an engaged person will speak of their soon-to-be spouse in glowing terms — all they are and all they do. On the other hand, married people can be prone to speak of their spouse in terms of what they are *not* and what they *fail* to do. Why do you think this is, and how can we work against such negativity when speaking of our spouse?

> *"Lord, how do I love my spouse today like they've never been loved before and never will be loved again?"*

8. Gary closed with the story of Brian and Haley. How does this true-life example of devotion and love put marriage into perspective?

9. As this study of *Sacred Marriage* comes to an end, what is one new outlook or action you will take away in terms of your marriage relationship?

CLOSING

Take time as a group (or as couples) to pray in some of the following directions:

- Creator God, you made men and women gloriously different. Teach us to see these differences as a gift, not a curse.
- Spirit of God, let our marriage be a laboratory for you to work in each of our lives, and teach us to love and serve like the Savior who gave himself for us.
- Give us eyes to see our spouse as you do, and not from our limited perspective.
- Lord Jesus, show us the folly of dreaming about some nonexistent "soul mate" and instead teach us to invest our heart, service, and love in the "sole mate" you have already given us.

IN THE COMING DAYS

COUPLE'S CONVERSATION AND PRAYER

Take time after this group meeting to talk and pray together about one or more of these topics:

- **Talk About It:** Talk with your spouse about one or two big lessons that hit you during the DVD and discussion time with your group. Consider how you can grow in your ability to humbly serve each other.

- **Pray About It:** Pray together for hearts that are willing to learn love in both good and hard times. Thank God for how he has forged you through your marriage relationship. Surrender your future together to God and ask for the strength to be devoted to your spouse for the rest of your life.

- **Read and Reflect:** Read John 19:1 – 37, one gospel writer's account of the ultimate example of service — Jesus' death on the cross. Talk together about how the sacrifice of Jesus can be an ever present reminder of how you are to love and serve one another.

ACTIVITIES

Try one or more of the following suggestions:

- **Personal Exercise:** Review the lists you created in response to question two (page 71). If you identify any unhealthy motives on the list that reflect your heart, identify how you need to adjust your perception of marriage with God's understanding of marriage.

- **Journaling Exercise:** *Take time to review your journal entries from sessions one through five, add any new insights, and highlight the three or four biggest lessons you have learned during the Sacred Marriage study (a page has been provided at the end of this session). If you've commited yourself to any new attitudes or actions, share these with your spouse and ask them to hold you accountable.*

- **Personal Prayer:** *Pray that the lessons you've learned over these six sessions will not be a short-term topic to think about, but will lead to a lifelong commitment to a biblical model of marriage.*

RECOMMENDED READING

Finish reading the book Sacred Marriage, *by Gary Thomas, if you haven't done so already.*

Journal

Sacred Marriage

What If God Designed Marriage to Make Us Holy More Than to Make Us Happy?

Gary Thomas

Your marriage is more than a sacred covenant with another person.

It is a spiritual discipline designed to help you know God better, trust him more fully, and love him more deeply.

Scores of books have been written that offer guidance for building the marriage of your dreams. But what if God's primary intent for your marriage isn't to make you happy … but holy? And what if your relationship isn't as much about you and your spouse as it is about you and God?

Everything about your marriage — everything — is filled with prophetic potential, with the capacity for discovering and revealing Christ's character. The respect you accord your partner; the forgiveness you humbly seek and graciously extend; the ecstasy, awe, and sheer fun of lovemaking; the history you and your spouse build with one another — in these and other facets of your marriage, *Sacred Marriage* uncovers the mystery of God's overarching purpose.

This book may very well alter profoundly the contours of your marriage. It will most certainly change you. Because whether it is delightful or difficult, your marriage can become a doorway to a closer walk with God, and to a spiritual integrity that, like salt, seasons the world around you with the savor of Christ.

Softcover: 978-0-310-24282-6

Pick up a copy today at your favorite bookstore!

Share Your Thoughts

With the Author: Your comments will be forwarded to the author when you send them to *zauthor@zondervan.com*.

With Zondervan: Submit your review of this book by writing to *zreview@zondervan.com*.

Free Online Resources at
www.zondervan.com

Zondervan AuthorTracker: Be notified whenever your favorite authors publish new books, go on tour, or post an update about what's happening in their lives at www.zondervan.com/authortracker.

Daily Bible Verses and Devotions: Enrich your life with daily Bible verses or devotions that help you start every morning focused on God. Visit www.zondervan.com/newsletters.

Free Email Publications: Sign up for newsletters on Christian living, academic resources, church ministry, fiction, children's resources, and more. Visit www.zondervan.com/newsletters.

Zondervan Bible Search: Find and compare Bible passages in a variety of translations at www.zondervanbiblesearch.com.

Other Benefits: Register yourself to receive online benefits like coupons and special offers, or to participate in research.

ZONDERVAN®

ZONDERVAN.com/
AUTHORTRACKER
follow your favorite authors